ENJOY THE MASS

Our Family Celebration
with Parent-teacher Notes

Jeannine Timko Leichner

Our Sunday Visitor Publishing Division
Our Sunday Visitor, Inc.
Huntington, Indiana 46750

Nihil Obstat: Rev. Lawrence Gollner / Censor Librorum

Imprimatur: ✠ William E. McManus / Bishop of Fort Wayne-South Bend / October 20, 1977

Cover designed by James McIlrath

Joy Joy, the Mass: Our Family Celebration

Address inquiries to:
Our Sunday Visitor, Inc.
200 Noll Plaza
Huntington, Indiana 46750

PRINTED IN THE UNITED STATES OF AMERICA

ISBN 0-87973-350-0

If you have ever been at Mass and wondered just what it is all about and why it seems so important, this little book is for you.

When I was born, I became a member of the

_____

family.

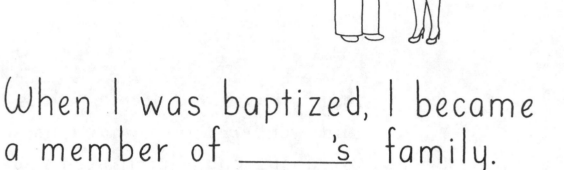

When I was baptized, I became a member of _____'s family.

Jesus invites God's family
to come together
to celebrate the Mass.

God's family is called the C_ _ _ _ _ _.

The Mass is a holy meal.

A meal should be a happy time when the family is at peace with one another and God. Sins destroy our peace. At the beginning of Mass, we ask forgiveness of God and each other so that we may really be one family.

I confess to almighty God,
and to you,
    my brothers and sisters,
that I have sinned
through my own fault
  _ in my thoughts
  _ and in my words,
  _ in what I have done,
  _ and in what I have
    failed to do;
and I ask blessed Mary,
ever virgin, all the angels
and saints, and you,
    my brothers and sisters,
to pray for me
to the Lord our God.

May almighty God have mercy
on us, forgive us our sins, and
bring us to everlasting life.
Amen.

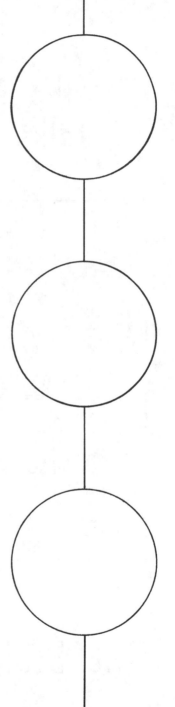

At the Mass, we talk to God our Father in our prayers.

At the Mass, God our Father talks to us in the readings.

The readings come from the _ _ _ _ _.

The Bible is the <u>word of God</u>.

The Lord be with you.
And also with you.
A reading from the holy gospel.
Glory to you, Lord.

We l_ _ _ _ _ carefully.

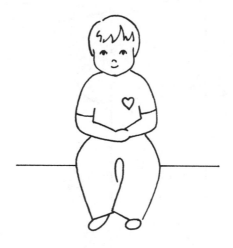

We try to u_ _ _ _ _ _ _ what
God is saying to us.

This is the gospel of the Lord.
Praise to you, Lord Jesus Christ.

The priest helps us understand what God is saying to us.

We call this part of the Mass the h_____.

We all belong to one family.
We pray for each other.

For_____

For_____

For_____

For_____

We pray to the Lord.

Lord, hear our prayer

At the Mass, we give thanks to God for all of the good things he has given us.

I want to thank God for

_____

_____

_____

We bring gifts to show our love
and thanks.

We bring b_____ and w_____.
We bring m_____.
We bring our l_____.

BLESSED BE GOD
FOR EVER

The priest prays that God will be pleased with our gifts and with us.

Then he prepares to do
what Jesus did
at the Last Supper.

Holy
Holy
Holy Lord

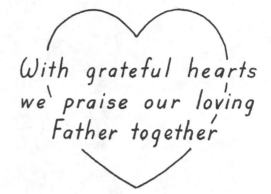

With grateful hearts we' praise our loving Father together

God of power and might,
Heaven and earth are full of your glory.
Hosanna in the highest.

Put a
beautiful
picture
here.

Blessed is he who comes in the name
of the Lord.
Hosanna in the highest.

Jesus said

_____ _____ _____ _____ _____ _____.

_____ _____ _____ _____ _____ _____.

Do this in

the Last Supper

The priest says

———— ———— ———— ————.

———— ———— ———— ————.

memory of me

Our gifts are changed into Jesus Himself!

We call Jesus' body and blood the Holy Eucharist.
Eucharist means t_____.

We offer this most wonderful gift to God with Jesus.

Through him,
with him,
in him,

in the unity of the Holy Spirit, all honor and glory is yours, Almighty Father, for ever and ever.

♪ AMEN ♫

Our Gift Becomes Our Food!

We prepare to receive Jesus in Holy Communion by praying together in the words he gave us...

Our _____, who art in heaven, hallowed be thy _____; thy kingdom come; thy will be _____ on earth as it is in heaven. Give us this _____ our daily bread; and forgive us our trespasses as we _____ those who trespass against us; and _____ us not into temptation, but deliver ____ from evil.

...and by sharing
his peace with
others.

Jesus loves me. He comes to me.

The priest says: Happy are those who are
    called to his supper.
We answer: Lord, I am not worthy to receive
    you, but only say the word and I shall
    be healed.

Jesus is very close to me. I talk to him.

Jesus said,
"I am the Bread of Life."

When Jesus comes to
us in Holy Communion
he helps us <u>grow in love</u>
for God and others.

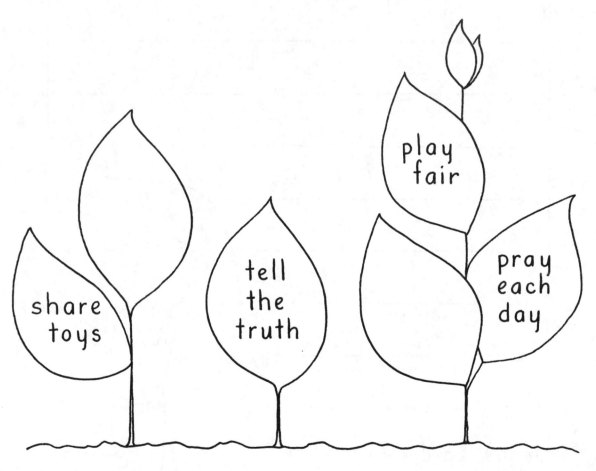

We are united with J_ _ _ _
and each o_ _ _ _.

We s_ _ _ _ his life and love.

The Mass is ended.

Go in peace
to love and serve the Lord.

T_____ be to God.

LOVE * LOVE * LOVE * LOVE

We leave Mass ready to share
Jesus' love with others.

At the Mass:

We come _____.

God _____ to us.

We talk to _____.

We offer _____ to God.

The _____ and _____ are
    changed into Jesus' body
    and blood.

_____ comes to us in Holy
    Communion. He _____ us.

When we leave Mass we want to
_____ Jesus' love with _____.

This is your special book.
You can take it to Mass
with you.

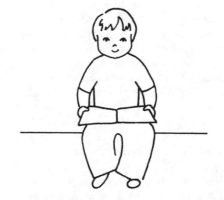

Notes for Parents and Teachers

Introduction

Most religion texts for primary grade children contain lessons on the Mass; but often something more is needed. This book offers a simple, activity-oriented presentation of the basic ideas of the Mass, with the hope that the children who use it will find it enjoyable and come to a better understanding of our family celebration, the Mass.

Although this book was designed for use by children in primary grades in a traditional CCD or parochial-school religion class, it can be a valuable supplement in a family program or can be used by itself in the home. Because of the simplicity of presentation, the book's topics can be expanded in many directions, as indicated in these Notes.

The Mass is a many-faceted experience, rich in meaning and interpretation. This book focuses on the meal aspect of the Mass, as an appropriate beginning for young children. The basic ideas are summed up in a few sentences accompanied by simple illustrations. The text and pictures are closely related to the experiences of children. Much of the message is conveyed pictorially, and time given to looking at the illustrations, discussing and coloring them, is well spent. Many pages have missing words, or places for the child to include personal thoughts or drawings. As the children complete these activities and color the pictures, the book becomes uniquely theirs. Brief prayers and responses from the liturgy of the Mass have likewise been included to familiarize the children with them, so that they can join the parish community at Mass with an increased sense of belonging.

When this book is used in a weekly class, the teacher should plan to extend its study over a period of several weeks, taking only a few pages at a time. As simple as the ideas presented in the book may seem, young children will find them very profound and will require time to assimilate them even in an elementary way. The whole of the weekly class-time need not be devoted to this book, however. It can be successfully interwoven with other pertinent lessons. When returning to the book or beginning a new section, the teacher is advised to review the previously completed pages.

An ideal way to conclude this study is to arrange a special children's Mass, in which the children can participate as fully as possible. Some of the text from the book can be used as oral commentary during the Mass, thus providing a meaningful link between the study of the Mass and the Mass itself. In any case, the children should be encouraged to take the completed book with them when they go to Mass. Following its pages can help strengthen and deepen their appreciation of the Mass as they join the other members of God's family in its celebration.

The brief notes that follow contain some background for the ideas presented on each page and suggest possible ways of amplifying the material and for approaching it with the children.

—J.T.L.

□

Page 4. When we were born, we were very special to our own family. We had our own little place and received a great deal of loving care and attention. In the same way, when we were baptized, the whole family of God took a special interest in us. Children need to see that Baptism extends our belonging. It unites us with people everywhere who accept God as their Father and Jesus as their Savior and Brother. We are truly brothers and sisters of each other and should learn to love and care for each other.

Missing words: (Family name), GOD.

Page 5. One of the important things we share as members of God's family is our special love for God, our Father. As individuals we may belong to different kinds of families and live in different kinds of houses; but at Mass we all come together at Jesus' call to express our one love for God. To help make this concept clear, have each of the children write the names of their own family, friends, neighbors, or relatives on the roofs of the houses. They can complete the picture by adding the name of their own church. The meaning of the word *church* on the bottom of this page may call for some discussion. The children are probably used to thinking of the word *church* only in connection with the building.

Missing word: CHURCH.

Activity: Write family names on house roofs, name of church on church roof.

Page 6. Two main concepts are presented here. The first is the idea that the Mass is a holy meal. It is truly the Lord's Supper, a commemoration of his Last Supper. The children can easily see that the physical setting—a table, cup, plate, and food—is similar. When we think about what happens at an ordinary meal, we discover that basically we talk, listen, and eat. At the Mass, the family of God gathers around the Lord's table to talk to God, listen to him, and be nourished by his Son, Jesus. The second idea is the importance of being at peace with one another before we begin. It may be helpful to have the children reflect upon an ordinary meal in their own experience when the members of their families were not at peace with each other. Just being together does not necessarily mean real togetherness. We need to resolve our differences, admit our shortcomings, and be willing to forgive others so that the peace of the Lord may come into our hearts. What better way to begin this wonderful celebration! (See Matthew 5:23-25.) To show the joy we experience when we forgive and are forgiven, the children can draw smiles on the faces of the boys and girls gathered around the altar.

Activity: Draw smiles on the children's faces.

Page 7. This prayer is our way of setting things right before we begin. Some of the ideas that can be readily explored with the children if time permits are: (1) When we sin, we need to ask forgiveness of God *and* our brothers and sisters. (2) Sin is not always what we do, but sometimes what we do not do. Give the children some examples to think about. (3) We ask for help in the form of prayers from the members of God's family here on earth, as well as from our great relatives in heaven, the saints. Be sure to discuss the meaning of the word *mercy* with the children.

Activity: Write "Lord, have mercy," "Christ, have mercy," "Lord, have mercy" in the three circles.

Page 8. The Liturgy of the Word can be informally viewed as the conversational part of the Mass as our holy meal. God is indeed speaking to us through the readings. This page presents a beautiful opportunity to talk about the Bible with the children. Show the children a Bible: explain its main parts; find the section from which a recent Sunday reading was taken; talk about the writers; and so forth. It is important to help the children understand that although the Bible was written long ago, it has meaning for us now.

Missing word: BIBLE.

Page 9. The Gospel is an especially important part of the readings. It is the word of God as revealed by his own Son, Jesus Christ. Jesus' message of love comes to us not only in his words, but also through his actions. Read a recent Sunday Gospel with the children and help them to discover in it what Jesus is saying to us today. In familiarizing the children with the responses before and after the Gospel (as well as others), it may be helpful to have them underline their parts.

Missing words: LISTEN, UNDERSTAND.

Activity: Underline "responses."

Page 10. It should be clear to the children, both from their own experience and from the discussions about the readings, that it is sometimes difficult to understand what God is saying to us. In the homily, the priest helps us understand God's message of love and how we can apply it to our daily lives. We do our part by listening carefully with open hearts and minds. (See Luke 8:4-15.)

Missing word: HOMILY.

Page 11. At the Mass, we are constantly reminded of our close relationship with other people. The prayers of petition should reflect our loving concern for others and their needs. In order to encourage the children to think about the needs of the other people in God's family, pictures of people in various situations could be shown to them and discussed with them. Another approach is to make a list, with the children's help, of the needs of different categories of people (parents, sick people, farmers, etc.) as a basis for their own prayers of petition.

Activity: Write petitions.

Page 12. Thanksgiving is a fundamental theme of the Mass. We thank God for the wonderful things he has given us, especially his Son, Jesus. It is important that the children be helped to recognize God's goodness to them personally so that they can appreciate the significance of the Offertory of the Mass. Looking at the picture on this page with them may help bring some of God's goodness to mind.

Activity: List things for which we are grateful.

Page 13. It seems natural for us to express deep thankfulness with a gift—think of Mother's Day and Father's Day. In the same way, we bring gifts to God in loving gratitude for his gifts to us. The bread and wine are symbolically the work of our hands; the money we contribute is a direct consequence of our efforts. Sharing what we have with others is a way of offering ourselves and our love to God. It might be worthwhile to spend a few minutes talking about what happens to the collection money, as an example of how the members of God's family show love and concern for each other. (See Matthew 25:34-40.)

Missing words: BREAD, WINE, MONEY, LOVE.

Page 14. The priest as our ordained representative accepts the gifts we bring to the altar and prays that God will be pleased with them and with us. The bread and wine have a special destiny; they will be changed into Jesus himself. The priest asks God to make them holy as he begins the prayers that lead to the actions of Jesus at the Last Supper. If the children are not yet aware of the events of the Last Supper, or their meaning, it is essential to share these things with them now so that they will be able to see the re-presentation of the Last Supper in the Mass.

Activity: Complete the letters in the response "BLESSED BE GOD FOR EVER."

Page 15. We learn about friends we cannot see by the letters they write and send us, or perhaps through the pictures they draw or the things they make. In the same way, we cannot see God, but we can look to his creations to help us know him—the power of the waves, a gentle breeze, the majestic mountains, a delicate flower in the sun, the radiant beauty of autumn leaves. All such things speak to us of God's greatness and glory. In joy we echo this song of praise, "Holy, holy, holy Lord, . . ." as a prelude to the important events that will soon take place in the Mass. An appropriate response to the ideas on this page is a brief prayer-service, during which each child mentions something that God has made, as seen in his own picture; and the group concludes

with the recitation of this beautiful hymn of praise.
Activity: Put a beautiful picture of nature in the space provided (something from a magazine, or a postcard).

Pages 16 and 17. Why have we assembled here together? To remember what the Lord has done for us, to celebrate the Lord's Supper. Jesus gave himself to his Apostles at the Last Supper when he changed bread and wine into his body and blood and gave both to them. This was to be a continuing sign of his love for all people. Jesus gives himself to us at the Mass when the priest takes bread and wine and repeats the words Jesus said at the Last Supper. Everything on these two pages is designed to point up the similarity between these two events. The children should be able to see that we are following Jesus' command, "Do this in memory of me," when we come together as a family at Mass.
Missing words: THIS IS MY BODY. THIS IS MY BLOOD.

Page 18. When the priest repeats Jesus' words, "This is my body . . . This is my blood," Jesus is made present in a special way among his family. The bread becomes his body. The wine becomes his blood. It is by *faith in Jesus* that we know he is present in the Eucharist, even though we still see and taste bread and wine.
Missing word: THANKSGIVING.

Page 19. At last we have the perfect gift for God our Father—Jesus himself. As he elevates Jesus' body and blood, the priest offers a prayer of highest praise to God. We respond in whole-hearted agreement by saying the great "Amen." The children should understand that the word *him* in the prayer on this page refers to Jesus. It is through Jesus, with Jesus, and in Jesus that we thank and praise God completely. The children can underline the word *him* to help emphasize its meaning.
Activities: Complete the picture, and underline the word *him* in three places.

Pages 20 and 21. God our Father lovingly shares the wonderful gift of his Son with us. In explaining this aspect of the Mass to children, a comparison can be made with a mother who receives a box of candy from her children and then shares the candy with them. We prepare ourselves to receive Jesus by turning again to our Father in prayer and to our brothers and sisters in peace and friendship. It may be helpful to write the missing words of the Our Father on the board in scrambled order. Before going on, point out to the children that "Holy Communion" and "Holy Eucharist" refer to the same thing.
Missing words: FATHER, NAME, DONE, DAY, FORGIVE, LEAD, US.
Activity: Write the usual greeting of peace.

Page 22. Jesus lived in one time and in one place. But his love for people did not stop then and there. He is with us now. In the Holy Eucharist, he comes to us in a special and personal way. He is the source of our strength and the brother in whom we confide. When the priest offers us the Body of Christ in Holy Communion, we answer, "Amen." The word *amen* expresses our belief that Jesus is present in the Holy Eucharist. It means, "Yes, I believe."
Activity: Write the words of the priest, "Body of Christ," and the girl's response, "Amen."

Page 23. When we receive Holy Communion, Jesus is with us in a closeness whose true nature escapes even the most profound thinkers. Nevertheless, this very closeness is what we want to communicate to the children. Jesus, who cares for us, is with us. Jesus, who listens, is with us. Jesus, who strengthens, is with us. Encourage the children to share their feelings, concerns, joys, etc., with Jesus when they return from Holy Communion. If the children are too young to write a prayer for the occasion individually, it may be desirable to compose a prayer together, with everyone helping; write it on the board, and then have them copy it as a model for their own prayer.
Activity: Compose a prayer to say after receiving Communion.

Page 24. Jesus comes to us as holy food, the Bread of Life. Ordinary food nourishes us, strengthens us, and helps us grow. Receiving Jesus in the Holy Eucharist helps us *grow in love*. Strengthened by this unique union, we can become more and more like Jesus as we go about our everyday affairs. Some of the ways children can grow in love, i.e., be like Jesus, are shown on the little plants. Help the children think of other ways, adding other leaves as needed. Encourage them to be specific.
Activity: Write other ways to grow in love, on the leaves.

Page 25. Our own union with Jesus in the Holy Eucharist is only part of the picture. The children should begin to recognize that our unity with Jesus draws us into an even closer relationship of love with our brothers and sisters in God's family, because Jesus is close to them, too. In other words, being close to Jesus in Holy Communion means being close to each other as well. A string of paper dolls may be helpful in explaining this idea to the children.
Missing words: JESUS, OTHER, SHARE.
Activity: Cut out paper dolls and put them in front of Jesus (or complete the outline-drawings).

Page 26. The Mass is over. We have come together as a family; we have shared in the Lord's Supper. When we are aware of our closeness to Jesus and each other, our hearts are filled with peace and joy. As we prepare to leave, we are urged to share this peace and joy with other people—at home, at school, at play, or wherever we go.
Missing word: THANKS.

Page 27. This page is very important. It gives the children the opportunity to make the vital connection between the Mass and their own daily lives. Jesus shows his love for us when he comes to us in Holy Communion. We share this same love with others when we see their needs and meet them. Jesus' love for us makes our love for others stronger. He is the vine, we are the branches. Have the children think about their own lives and how they could be kind or helpful to someone else. Have them draw a picture of one of the ways, inside the frame.
Activity: Draw a picture in the frame showing a way to share Jesus' love with others.

Page 28. The book concludes with a few simple sentences to be completed by the children. These are meant not so much as a test, as an opportunity for the children to bring together for themselves the key ideas of the Mass. For young children, it is best to write the answer choices on the board in scrambled order. "Correcting" the completed answers in class can provide additional review or clarification. Let the children correct any mistakes they may have made so that they may complete their book with a feeling of satisfaction.
Missing words: TOGETHER, TALKS, GOD, GIFTS, BREAD, WINE, JESUS, LOVES, SHARE, OTHERS.